LYNDA

VERGE

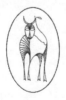

*for Cathy
with love,
Lynda*

GUERNICA

TORONTO — BUFFALO — LANCASTER (U.K.)
2015

Copyright © 2015, Lynda Monahan and Guernica Editions Inc.
All rights reserved. The use of any part of this publication,
reproduced, transmitted in any form or by any means, electronic,
mechanical, photocopying, recording or otherwise stored in a
retrieval system, without the prior consent of the publisher is an
infringement of the copyright law.

Michael Mirolla, general editor
Dave Margoshes, editor
Guernica Editions Inc.
1569 Heritage Way, Oakville ON (Canada) L6M 2Z7
2250 Military Road, Tonawanda, N.Y. 14150-6000 U.S.A.

Distributors:
University of Toronto Press Distribution,
5201 Dufferin Street, Toronto (ON), Canada M3H 5T8
Gazelle Book Services, White Cross Mills, High Town, Lancaster LA1 4XS U.K.

Typesetting by Antonio D'Alfonso.
First edition.
Printed in Canada.

Legal Deposit – First Quarter
Library of Congress Catalog Card Number: 2014950182
Library and Archives Canada Cataloguing in Publication
Monahan, Lynda, 1952-, author
Verge / Lynda Monahan. — First edition.
(Essential poets series ; 223)
Poems.
Issued in print and electronic formats.
ISBN 978-1-55071-963-5 (pbk.).
ISBN 978-1-55071-964-2 (epub).
ISBN 978-1-55071-965-9 (mobi).
I. Title. II. Series: Essential poets series ; 223
PS8576.O45182V47 2015   C811'.54 C2014-906228-1
C2014-906229-X

contents

*for Don, Shawn, Jill, Josh, Connor and Kyle
and for my sister, Patti, beautiful as the first morning*

the fox spirit is the great problem solver — she will guide you to solitude and silence until the way out is shown

Spirit Animals

verge 1

I said to the wanting-creature inside myself
what is this river you wish to cross

and a small fox spoke to me then
from the shadows by the old road

the river holds the past
the sweep of its long sadness

it is the cold yesterday
of our childhood

and with my eyes
the small fox smiled at me

now come she said it is time
we swim to the other side...

in the beginning

our hearts were seeds
our parents stitched
in thin acidic soil

like a small wound
my brother's opened
sent out a frail shoot
pale thing
that yellowed
then withered
and died

my sister's split in half
and grew two different ways
from such hard pruning
too much cutting back
and too much
lack
of everything

and mine took root
a dark and twisted thing
that bent and polished
fought toward the sun
and flowered there

among the roses
where you made
a place for me

all the words

I can peel an orange
all in one piece
apples too   a trick my brother taught me
to roll an orange in my palm
poke a hole with my forefinger
suck the juice out through a straw

we played catch with Christmas oranges
made parachutes from the green tissue
they came nestled in
loved the strange symbols
on the wooden box
traced them carefully onto paper

all the words we wanted to
but couldn't say

the ironing

the air is stunned by noon heat
and the slammed door of dad's leaving
the old ironing board set up
in the crowded kitchen
wicker basket filled to overflowing
mom in pedal pushers
and a sleeveless blouse
her hair small x's of bobby pins

steam hissing up
as she places a damp tea towel
a flex of her slim wrist
as she slicks the iron back and forth
over the width of dad's white work shirts
the stiff arch of his collar

fold and press and flip and fold and press
the red transistor radio singing its promises

that's okay Rose would say
don't you worry none
we'll have good times by and by
next fall when the work's all done

the hush of her soft voice
as she irons creases
sharp as knives into dad's black dress pants
the way she comforts herself with song

stars of blood

every autumn
a week off work
to hunt deer at MacDowall
he came home triumphant
a young buck slung limp
pale bellied and marble eyed
in the back of George's half ton truck
a ritual
we'd all go out to admire the kill
then haul it unceremoniously down the stairs
where it hung like heartbreak
from a rope in the basement
stars of blood congealing on the concrete floor

or it was an elk or a moose
shot up north
or an antelope down south
ducks and prairie chickens
plucked in the kitchen sink
wood partridge and the gone grace
of Canada geese   their long necks dangling

he brought them all home
our house thick with the coppery
scent and taste   the rich glint of it
like gold in father's eyes
on our walls
the antlers and deer hoof gun racks
hung like dark medallions
of some battle he'd fought and won

my mother's name was Nancy

she wore red lipstick pinched her cheeks
to give them colour
after the war mom met a young French man
who broke her heart
later she married dad in a long satin gown
fifty tiny buttons down her back

***

her favourite sister was the oldest Jessie
not long before mom died she visited her in Toronto
she bought two new dresses
one a butter yellow the other bright blue
mom was buried in the yellow dress
the one she liked best

***

she grew glorious roses
lush gardens of fat vegetables
her cold room shelves lined
with gem jars of canned crab apples
sewed red velvet dresses for my sister and me
short pants for our brother
made her own mastectomy bras
stuffing them with old stockings

***

she kept four geese
Herman and Hector Pansy and Petunia
they'd stampede up the driveway
and we'd make a run for the door
closing it fast on their snapping beaks
they adored mom though
coming when she called
rubbing their wings against her legs

***

she loved wandering the woods back of our house
made bottle gardens from moss and seedlings
sold them in the craft shop at the lake
miniature replicas of the Nisbet Forest
the place that was her home

***

she baked terrible pies using margarine in the crust
wonderful cakes from her best friend's recipe
Coo Clark's Crazy Chocolate Cake
she liked Readers Digest condensed versions
big leathery brown volumes
special ordered through the mail
lost herself in stories like The Slow Awakening
curled in an armchair in a pool of lamplight
head tilted to one side

***

she learned to drive in her forties
stalled the car
in the middle of second avenue once
thought it was my fault because I closed the ashtray
she never took a drink
wouldn't dance seldom missed church
and that was the one time I heard her say *damn*

***

when she lost her hair she wore a brown wig
squeezed a rubber ball to help her regain strength
in her arms though it never returned
she could hardly lift a thing
but she climbed up and fixed the eaves
on the house and when she did
dad wouldn't speak to her for three days

***

she stayed home as long as she could
showing me how to make seven layer dinner
when to add the fabric softener
two weeks before Christmas
in the middle of the night

Dr. Martinson came saying
Nancy it's time we took you to the hospital now
and she hesitated then her quiet voice answered him *yes*

a bitter sun

I am riding the bus to Saskatoon
this blustery January afternoon
highway a spin of ice
wind dancing the snow up around
and into the frozen sky where sundogs
bracket the distant orb
like an afterthought
messengers of a deep and holding cold

around me the quiet conversations of my fellow travellers
red haired woman in front of me deep in a Harlequin
     romance
smell of stale cigarettes and Cheezies
the bus's constant kathump bump over the ridges of snow

I think of my mother who rode the bus all those years ago
back and forth to the city for her chemo treatments
did she look out at the same gray and white world
and wonder if she would ever see it warm again
those long rides those days of dangerous wind chills
left to memory the fields at last greening
sun's warmth soft on her shoulders

did she lean her tired head against the window
as I do now a brown bag with a cheese sandwich
and a polished apple left uneaten on the seat beside her
her checked car coat folded neatly across her lap

did she sit looking out at the killing cold
fighting back nausea all the way home
the cancer cells already dividing and growing inside her
deceptive as this bright but bitter sun

edge of the season

the winter mom died
Christmas was tinny music on the radio

garish lights on the icy streets
so bright we wept

there were no gifts that year

cards lined the china cabinet
not one read *Happy Holidays*

we lived on the edge of the season

loss like lumps of coal
beneath our nonexistent tree

verge 2

I imagine you out there
in the cool breath of forest
among the green black pines
always you run in my blood
fiery with your truths
and the song of my longing

small fox so much wiser you are than I
you understand life
while I only stumble along
seeking your serenity
your quiet life

what gifts you have
what amazing treasures
do you know
I would trade all my lovely things
for your good grace...

photograph

the five year old boy will always be there
on the wooden dock at the Heart Lakes
wearing his Waskesiu sailor hat and shorts
grinning hard for the camera

his sister will always be there
right next to him
her blonde hair in ribboned braids
her face turned even then toward shadows

in an old album on the closet shelf
they will always be this way
she will hold her brother's hand forever
as if she won't ever have to let him go

salt

there is no adequate word
for how it felt the day you died
no adequate way to say how I knew
no answers to any of the questions
I had or why poems spilled out of me
in a great sweep of guilt and sorrowing

no name for the glittering white fury
I heaped on our father or for the loss I felt
and still feel over you little brother
my friend and protector

how to put words to my missing you
real as the salt I poured and poured
into the open wound of your leaving
only now beginning at last to heal

four generations

fists on her hips
grandmother demands
we pose for this photo
dad glares into the camera
arms crossed
next to him I sit stiff backed

only my small son
who knows what is expected of him
grins

of love

my mother died
a bud
a tight pink rose
that could not bloom

my father died
a hollow room
he barred the door
let no-one in

my brother died
scarred snow blind
a field of white inside him

but no-one
there is no-one in my family
who ever died of love

through my father's eyes 1

where's the damn line   nobody ever showed me
thought maybe I'd found it once   that line
then Nance getting cancer
all that back and forth to Saskatoon
and then she died   she just died

and those kids looking at me
like I should have the answers
should find the line for them
when I couldn't even find it for myself

the boy he was always going way over the line
finally finding no way back
and the girls were always wanting
and I didn't know what

if you ask me   if you want my opinion
that line should be drawn out in big black marker
then maybe we'd know where the hell it is
we're all supposed to be

my father taught me

to grow rage
to watch the gauge
inside me
rising
until it all gave way
spattering everything
with its hot white burning

he taught me to
keep it festering there
how to feed it small bites
to keep it hungry
keep it fierce and full

taught me to hold it
caged and pacing
fiery eyed and ready to rip
into anyone who might
reach
out a hand to touch me

through my father's eyes 2

they insist
on coming into my room
every five minutes
checking I suppose
to see if I'm still kicking

sometimes I open my eyes a bit
see the oldest standing in the doorway
look on her face
like she wants to say something

I just shut my eyes
pretend I'm sleeping
I don't want her words
don't want a thing
but to get this dying over with

the youngest one
comes on in anyway
plunks herself down on my bed
looks at me hard
till I do open my eyes

they bring me peaches
ice cream rice puddings
try to get me to eat
what do I need to eat for
I ask them

why won't they just leave me alone
the two of them
they tell me they love me
well what the hell am I supposed to say to that

dad's angel

no Billy Graham angel
all glory and grace
no heavenly host
to carry him away
no hallelujah

dad's angel
smoked a pack a day
wore a three day beard
a Blue Jays ball cap

dad's angel
kept Playboy magazines
hidden beneath the bed
drank beer with his buddies
loved the heft of a good gun

he didn't hold dad in his arms
when the time came
didn't smile a beatific smile

dad's angel just showed up
said *c'mon Bill let's go*

those words

(for Helen)

she remembers when her father died
that hard twist of emotion
relief braiding itself into sorrow
glad she was to have the vigil over
so sad to see him gone

she remembers when her father died
how she wished she'd said I love you
but she couldn't find those words for him
and how she'd wished he'd had those words for her
but he couldn't find them either

and she remembers the exhaustion
of long hospital days and nights
all that was her father gone
transmuted into that body on the bed
the barely discernible rise and fall of his last breathing

and here memory blossoms back
to when his arms were young and strong
and he'd lift her up to touch the ceiling
asking *whose little girl are you*

and her heart still holds the answer

there was a time

I was a thin walking stick of pain
carausius morosus
like the insect
wearing my exoskeleton
living on lettuce leaves

two days without food
sometimes three
the lighter I became
the less weighted I felt
to the fear of my family
their heavy chains loose
around my bird ankles
the impossibly small bones of my wrists

food pulled me down
into the overfull lap
of my father and grandmother
fat with disapproval

I wanted rid of their cruel excess
to be slender as a blade of blue-eyed grass
a will-o-the-wisp woman
or a wand   a magic wand
I could tap three times
make myself disappear

touching silence

they called my cousin deaf and dumb
she learned to sign
her slender hands shaping figures
in a ballet all their own

Lynn lived beyond the boundaries of speaking
people's faces so filled with meaning
the way their bodies sharpened into a language
so clear she had no need of hearing

she touched silence in a way I longed to
but never could   words clattered in my ears
scattered inside me like flung stones
that left too many bruises

I wanted to be Lynn
wrapped in a hush deeper than fallen snow
with only her hands turning and turning
in the silent dance of all she had to say

seven syllables

how musical those words are
malignant melanoma
tropical parrot feather words
their rainforest drumbeat rhythm
like a dance
the salsa   the mamba   the melanoma

colourful and exotic
sound of those seven syllables
rare as jungle songbirds

but this is no song
my sister sings
no merengue that she swings her hips to

there is no warmth to those words   no beauty
cold and clinical as this cancer
they remove and remove
their scalpels red with her blood

I wish it was a song   a dance
something beautiful I could make for her
from those two words
something worth living for

I have lost

mother father brother
I have lost
love friends beauty
I have lost joy

I have lost much
and I have counted those losses
carefully saved them
added and re-added them
the way the wealthy do their riches
the way my father did his pain

and I have held those losses
close as children
I have stroked their heads fondly
spoke their names in dreams
I have nurtured my losses
watched them grow until
they were so much bigger than me

I have let those losses
elbow their way
for more space in my heart
let them have whatever they wanted
I have spoiled my losses
I have given them every occasion

listen my sad children
it is long past time
I must release you now
look there is the open door
and here is my heart
bright with farewell

verge 3

small fox at the water's edge
every nerve in your bright body
elongated poised to leap
into the river's deep mysteries

what is it holds you there
lingering on that verge
what is it keeps you
from finding the other side

is it the future you fear
or the past you hold onto
that hiding you cannot
and do not wish to let go

listen little creature
to what I am telling you
go with your heart's hard pull

the river is singing
its small white song ...

before there was fire

before there was fire there was kindling
tinder dry asleep on the forest floor
there was a distant thunderhead
ominous on the far horizon

there was the fury of her father
tongue print of an anger
with nowhere to go but in
her heart was a lump of coal
a small and fisted thing

and when there was that first wisp
that first tendril of smoke
she uncurled her small fingers and grew

into the wanting of a small girl
for what she could never have
the desire of a woman that could not stop

a red dress that smoothed bare shoulders
there was a slow dance   a look
deep as dark eyes and she smouldered there
a loss there was and another and another
pain there was and sorrowing
a fever unconstrained
a beauty with consequence

and when she opened herself at last to flame
she climbed the shape of her imaginings
into the dark carved sky
and she lit her own way into the night

woman burning

kick off the covers
fling my gown into the dark

I glow   am pure heat
the colour red
an element left on high

a white hot shiver I am
a lit cigarette smoking

your arm across my waist
is too heavy too hot
your breath on my back
this room is a sauna

throw open the windows
I am a woman
burning up the night

when the river ran deep

we were newlyweds then when the river ran deep
all August we swam its ruffled waters
we'd roast wieners on willow sticks
drink cups of lime Kool-Aid

we'd stay slow afternoons
laid out on towels above the riverbank
listening to grasshoppers hum the summer heat

thirty years ago that was
our old swimming hole long since dried up
the banks shoulder high in couch grass
can hardly recognize where we once
lay long hours in the sun

I caution my grandsons about broken beer bottles
disposable diapers at the shallow water's edge
they tore down the old bridge years ago
where you'd balance on the concrete arches
that curved high over the river
a simple overpass now

time has taken this place
that holds no trace of who we once were
the river runs deep only in memory

no bridge left to carry us back

feeling the heat

we were a country of red earth
and molten lava
     my body arched
beneath yours   the air rushed with flames
in the hot kiss of all that making

when did we stop
     feeling the heat
when did we become like a photograph
of that country   where nothing moves
and nothing really burns

and I

an uneasy sky today
clouds dark and low
the pines hoar-frosted
a black and white world

you are a black and white world
either this way or that
no half way no grey
with you it's so simple
a yes or a no

and I am always so maybe
caught in that middle ground
between darkness and light

with me nothing is sure
the way it all is for you
written in stone

everything's what might be
a sigh   with me everything's
an uneasy sky

go ahead disappoint me

say drink all the diet pop you want
Aspartame be damned
make me a good strong pot of coffee

leave every light on in the house past midnight
turn up the heat
so I can run around the house
barefoot in my bathing suit
let the taps drip madly
           let them drip

don't tuck the sheets in so tight my toes curl
let's sleep all in a heap
my body flung sideways over yours

order jerk chicken for the two of us
why don't you
           no more bland anything

love is not

love is not level
it comes in degrees
like the thermometer
outside your kitchen window

love is not mathematical
the equation doesn't always balance
no matter what Mr. Selinger said
in grade nine algebra class

you cannot plan love
like a trip to Connecticut
to visit your sister

or organize it
like a grocery list
put it into compartments
fruits and vegetables
canned goods   baking needs

you can't make love behave
you can't even teach it to stay

Melissa Nancy

was the name we chose
all those years ago   the papers signed
two weeks and we would have you
infant girl

we'd readied your room
with red checked curtains
painted a cradle
your closet hung with tiny things

but I was so not well
so fragile
I couldn't care for me back then
how could I care for you

and so we cancelled you
cancelled you like a subscription to a magazine
we no longer wanted
like an appointment we couldn't keep
but my heart has never cancelled you
never given you away

I think of you sometimes   bright girl
picture you tossing your summer hair
see the gift of your easy smile
the way you'd like to laugh
your voice deep as memory

and I wonder if whoever took you
loved you as I so wanted to
I am the mother you never had
you will never know
how close we came

eclipse

night returns to our days
air suffused with this dying light

blackened out
like in times of war

an eclipse people once believed
was the finish of everything

is that what this darkening is
the apocalypse of us

you and I
at the end of the world

you see

you want to keep the tree up
long past Christmas time
and I am longing to toss it
out back with seed balls for the birds

you see the new growth
at the tips of branches   that bright greening
and I see rust dusted inner boughs
all of that dying   fallen needles
I'll be the one to sweep

you see the happy lights
bright ornaments
want the seasonal joy to last
and I want back to normal

but you'll kill it you say
and I answer *it's already dead*

verge 4

small fox you dream the sleep of changes
this turning time

I save my breath
counting the slow hours

I am leaving something of me behind
let it come you say
as it will

in the light of dawn
we meet again
at the surface

night after night
you take me with you
across the distance into dreams ...

buffalo narrows

out here the woods are dusky with bears
I inhale the musky breath of low bush cranberries

poplars dropping
their gold coins to the ground

a tall spruce
leans its great weight against the sky

the day nudges its way toward night
and I am small beyond any words

graffiti

through thick snow
I walk by the river
this late November afternoon
finding your footprints
where they step off into whiteness

and there on the concrete arches
of the Shell River Bridge
where you drew a dark haired girl
you left a dark scrawl

no-one has seen you
and beneath the bridge
the river is a sheet of dark water
scrawled with thin ice

I don't know
who or where you are
but I can't forget
your words are all they've found
they leave their white breath in me

first frost

I am not drawn
to the fiery bite
of chili peppers
not enticed
by spice these days

too bright too filled with light
sun scented tomatoes
in the hot fields
all that ripeness

I'd rather winter mint
fragrant in the dark forest
the lick of first frost
or a silver drink of river

clean tasting shady flavours
for my quickly cooling heart

in this last light

the sky a thin grey quilt
that does little to keep out
the plummeting chill

the brown trees tremble
cold earth pulling into itself
sheen of ice on the small sloughs
rant of a rough-edged wind

summer seems so long ago
sun splashed mornings of our youth
winter on the lip of this day
tripping toward us

in this last light
shadows are everywhere
time slanting away

and yet

here in this place
where mist swirls
like cream in stirred tea
above the dark cedars
where bull kelp
bobbing just off shore
wash up on wet black rocks
like prehistoric creatures from the deep

I am a woman
from a province locked by land
where the sea is neither dream nor memory
a place where oceans are wheat fields
rolling golden in an autumn wind

and yet I hold this rocking sea
its rawness in my bones
I have known that wild dark thrashing
what's swept up on the shore
I understand the sea's fierce heart
its life   its poetry

then

I would not
have gone with you
in the day's cold light
when the sky was bleached
of shadows
and the sun honest as salt

not when the world
was a clear
and uncomplicated place
and my eyes saw so well
all that was around me

but when the moon hung
low in a liquid sky
when the night air was soft
and longing lived
in my every cell
and the loons called
and called across the dark waters

when memories sang
along my skin
and there was a sigh to everything
oh if you'd have asked me
then

verge 5

you came to me
curious about this woman
wandering your forest
with her bucket of blueberries

a snap of twig
and I looked up
surprised to see you there

and you were a frenzy of beauty
then suddenly gone
but in that one bright instant
we recognized ourselves
we knew each other's name ...

is it

we must be careful
on the highway

there are deer
along the ditches·

is it like that
when you see me

there could be
a collision

you might not
turn in time

rolling red

even when you stand still
things begin to happen
the room doing its slow roll

a rolling red
New York drivers call it
if no-one is coming
they just slow down
go right on through

outside the window
the climbing rain reminds me of you
stoplights change to race car red

if you move
I can't stop what happens next
it's all green light with me   all go

even when you stand still
things begin to happen
your eyes are a special occasion
the room waits rolling

all night in the empty streets
the stoplight's steady rhythm

and there's nothing out there
there's nothing out there
but rain

not I

who writes these poems
not I   it's the fire woman
who turns and turns
in the shiver of silver flames
words sparking from her lips

who writes these poems
this wanton woman
undulating in the flames
desire dancing around her
licking her arms   her long hot neck

who writes these poems
this incendiary
tall flick of a woman
casting the heat of her words
into the dark of old nights

the wrong kind

she loved him
as certain dark things
are meant to be loved
recklessly and without thought

listening to her body's slow urge
toward him   hot and unruly
as a young girl's pulse

wanting to have the wrong kind of love
the kind her mother wouldn't approve of
her father would never allow

a bad leather clad motorcycle riding
kind of love   the kind that smokes
sexy as Jimmy Dean's eyes

starfish poem

a starfish has no brain
no nerve endings no synapses
feels nothing at all
let me be this blissfully unaware

let me be a starfish
a blue starfish
like the one we found in Rarotonga
floating along
bathed in blue water

nothing matters to a starfish
not even you

the cure for fire

(a primer)

on holidays visit Alaska   the Arctic Circle
dream frost engulfing you like flame

ditch your desires
don't even light that candle any more

give up on poetry
learn the art of sculpting snow

and don't keep kindling   especially truths

write this on the blackboard
one hundred times   virtuous

keep the sun from your body
let your limbs turn pale as lavender

forget salsa   the mamba
Latinos in tight pants

learn to enjoy a good blizzard
and love only men who like the colour blue

closing in

loneliest almost evening
time of day
night already on the air
licking its lips
stretching out its long length

I still can't say your name
without my heart's quick hunger
the hunger night knows

wolves nuzzling your collarbones
the darkness closing in

ceremony

my friend says we need a ceremony to bury you
symbolically of course because you're very much alive
just not to me

nothing fancy you understand no expensive accoutrements
I've already spent far too much of me
on you

there should be wine though at least for me
my friend doesn't drink any more

she's smart enough to deal with her addictions

and this ceremony is her idea
because she is trying to help me
handle mine

still

*the memory of you
emerges from the
night around me*

Pablo Neruda

so that you will hear me
I write these words
they take me back
to what was once love
cup your ear
as you stand listening to the still of morning
I am there with you whispering of old wants

***

tonight I can write the saddest lines
there is no joy in me
though I search through the long hours
there is only my want of you
over and over
like a child at the chalkboard
I must write you a thousand times

***

the light wraps you in its mortal flame
but in the dark
I saw you as something else
a perfection a pure desire
faultless as that
only when the light came
could I see you
as wholly human
flawed and mortal as myself

***

the same night whitening the same trees
we of that time are no longer the same
I am mending and you
I imagine quite whole
though the one time I saw you
your eyes were ragged
I felt my heart's quick rending
and I wondered if what we once had
could be undone in you still

***

white bee you buzz in my soul drunk with honey
and flight winds in slow spirals of smoke
I heard you inside me
the sweet buzz of you
the slow death spiral of my desire
my heart humming and drunk with you
so long to find my way sober

★★★

leaning into the afternoons I cast my sad net
toward your oceanic eyes
I catch no bright reflections
no silver leaping
my net holds only yesterdays
their plenty their lost shine

★★★

almost out of the sky half of the moon
anchors between two mountains
I do not belong here
I am what the forest makes
of its green breathing
you are neither here nor there
whether I belong or not
I can have no you

***

thinking tangling shadows in the deep solitude
how do I unknot the past
untie you from my memory
let the long rope of your body
unbind me from those shadows
let sunlight come trembling through the trees

***

the morning is full of storm
and in the heat of summer
I remember your skin's glisten
my heart's hard hammer
and everywhere the small bells of rain

***

girl lithe and tawny
oh I was her then
flashing my brown limbs for you
who desired the length of my gold legs
the caramel of my nipple's kiss
caught between your lips

***

drunk with pines and long kisses
the length of your body against mine
in the naked night
the only word was no
tears waist deep around me

***

we have lost even this twilight
only day to darkness now
no in-between time
of gentle hours
of quiet talk and laughter
there is only what is
and what has been

***

I have gone marking the atlas of your body
with crosses of fire
and you gave yourself
opened your shirt
touched that place where your heart rests
and I pressed my small brand
deep into your flesh

***

every day you play with the light of the universe
your choice whether gray skies or sun
that much power you held over me
the fires bloomed everywhere in this forest
and they were all of your making

***

I remember you as you were in that last autumn
dark and lovely and a sadness in you
I understood as my own
I remember you among the falling leaves
the only colour to our goodbye

***

I like for you to be still
it is as though you were absent
and without speaking without seeing
finally you fade from me
it is when your words reach my ears
and your eyes are upon me
that the air has sharp edges
and I am cut through

***

oh vastness of pines murmur of waves breaking
it is there along the shores of the lake
I love so well
I healed from you
the small voices of that wilderness
bringing me truth
the wind and rain washing you away from me
making me clean

* The first lines of each of these verses is from Neruda's *Twenty Love Poems and a Song of Despair.*

verge 6

small fox   your spirit
is like the slow fires of autumn
I see you turning
looking back at the year
the fields and the journeys
and looking ahead to ice and snow
and a way to cross that river...

the snow has come early this year

too late now to save the herbs
I meant to bring indoors
under the cover of snow
rosemary sage and bee balm
die their small deaths

too late I save nothing
not even myself these days
though I mean to
bring myself in before
the winter hits
before everything piles up
burying me
like the greying leaves of oregano
beneath that snow

the delicate dead flowers of thyme

the guest

on this quiet evening
I am my own guest
having invited myself in
made myself comfortable
in the good chair
with my warmest comforter
and a glass of wine

hello I say
how are you
we haven't spoken
in far too long

it's a bit awkward
this visit
there are usually so many others
it feels strange
to be entertaining no-one but me

busy she says *no time*
she looks like she might
leap up at any minute
I see her checking her list
the clock
impatiently tapping her toes

sit for a while I tell myself
but she isn't listening
I have to go she says

gulping her wine
throwing off the comforter

this has been great
thanks so much
got to run

then she is off again
and I am left
with her empty glass
held in my hands

at last

(for Greig)

old friend   in all your life
I wrote not a single poem for you
in nearly four decades of friendship
not a single poem

now we carry to the kitchen
your untouched tray
the last meal you did not have
wash the cold soup into the sink
garbage the grapes and salad
the wilted marigold in the small blue vase
meant to cheer you

we look through albums now
gather memories for your funeral
all the years of holidays we shared
Bermuda beaches
skiing the shores of a frozen Lake Louise
godparents to each other's children

how young we were
how beautiful back then
so much promise there was to everything
the trips   the talks   building your cabin at Carwin

so much I should have put to poems
but here it is   a single marigold in a blue vase
and here you are   in a poem
at last

deep enough

(for Shawn)

(after "The Faces of Deer" by Mary Oliver)

when for too long
I do not go deep enough into the woods
I lose heart
lose my way in the world

the tall pines ground me
give me peace
the river with its onward
never give up attitude
flowing always forward
up and over the hurdles
the beaver haul in its way

and the delicate shapes of deer
at the lip of the clearing
singing to me with their soft eyes
the sun strewn trails
that rise to the high ridge
where I look out over the tops of trees
where the crumbling log bench
someone built long ago
gives me a chance to rest
after the long climb

god lives there
at least the one I know
the god of wide open wonder
and when I go deep enough
I find myself again
and I bring all of me back home

meditation on blue

a bohunk colour grandma called it
I loved it anyway
painted my walls Tuscany blue
my blue Mikado dishes   aqua crystals
strung from the chandelier

blue is the colour of memory
in a dress my mother made
I slow danced with the boys
while the band played *she wore blue velvet*
I swore they sang that song only for me

and blue is the colour of loss
my brother's winter death
where he lay in a frozen field
snow falling all around him
in the bluest blue of night

the colour of love blue is
long smoky Rarotonga nights
rattan ceiling fan circling shadows
over our bed   silverblue moonlight
singing on my skin

blue the colour meant for boys
I never was a pink person
too apple pie happy a colour for me
there's an integrity to blue
its true blue is
it doesn't pretend to be something
the way chartreuse does or orange

inside me too
these shades of blue
from dark as a moonless midnight
to sheer as spring ice on the Shell River
cool and calm and more than a little melancholy
blue has good weight
there's a heaviness to blue
I was born to it
a colour I understand

concrete

these days she is drawn
to the cemetery
where her family lives

touches the etching of their names
David   Annie   William
Nancy   Daniel
speaks those names out loud
a litany of loss

she wonders
if they know she's here
if they remember her name
it's me she tells them

mother she tries the word *mom*
remembers dark hair and brown eyes
what else
it's been too many years for details

write what's concrete she tells her classes
and that's all that's here really
cement and stone

from where she stands

she sees him on her morning walks
a man tenting on a sandbar
stretching warm and soft
along the edge of the river
just him and his horse
framed by stands of jack pine
their green branches
shifting in the summer breeze

from where she stands
on the far bank
she sees long muscled arms
a terra cotta tan
hair loose about his shoulders
sometimes she sees him sitting there
cross legged in front of his tent
looking out over the river
other times combing the horse's sun filled mane

she wonders about this man
about his being there solitary by the river
what drew him to this place
does he know
about the curve just ahead
where the water tumbles cool and sweet
runs like threads of silk
through her fingers

or the way the sand feels
so firm beneath her feet
along the steep north bank

has he found the inukshuk
she built one weeping afternoon
from river rocks
to mark her old dog's passing
does he contemplate the trees at night
and what does he think of all that sky
awash with stars like spilled sugar

does he understand the way the river moves
like a giant secret
running green and clear and cold
has he cried to the river she wonders
as she has so often done
does he know all the anger and sadness
all the love her river holds

verge 7

little watcher you have taught me
how to shape shift
when the leaves no longer linger

to become like you
a sister to the snow...

the word for everything

sometimes it is necessary
to re-teach a thing its loveliness
                                        Galway Kinnell

1

the stroke has muddied my sister
made her unclear

I will tell and retell her
in words and in touch
until every tiny bud
in her stricken brain unfolds
with the knowledge of her loveliness

I will sing to her
the lullaby of her lost self
I will sing soft voiced and smiling
until everything for her is possible again

I will tell and retell her
until she understands
crystal bell clear
as these northern lakes
clear to the very core of her
that she is lovely

until her bones know it
until the blood memory
of all that is my sister
comes back to her to me

***

these first days she cannot find herself
in the long unmarked hours
of her mind's constant turning

adrift in the hospital
she fears the nurses doctors
trusts no-one

my son writes
on the chalkboard in her room
Shawn was here you are safe
pins his picture to the wall

she touches his face in the photograph
again and again she repeats his words
Shawn was here you are safe

***

as water
will
when hindered
she is
shaping
a new path

she will
carve
her way
as water will
through
stone

***

this sister is other
than the one I know
she lives beyond her old self
the one that was

she is
here   but not here
before   and after
then   and now
a present absence

the stroke has cut her life
cleanly   in half
like two sides of a green apple

***

she calls to ask me about herself
do I like Chinese food
she asks
do I like Star Trek

yes I say
or maybe
try it I tell her
you might

she trusts me
to tell her the truth

a guest
in her own home now
one she is trying to entertain

***

when will I be myself again

the question turns and turns inside the dark swirl of her
    thinking

time is unmade for her now   the future a mystical
landscape of distant blue shapes as indistinct as dreaming

when will I be myself again the question turns and turns

the answer is a scatter of slow moving stars
a fleck of light that cannot be calculated

a clatter of stones against the broken window of her sky

★★★

bent over her colouring books
she concentrates
outlines the blonde tresses of a princess bride
crayoning so carefully
she creates a world that keeps inside the lines

the roses she colours
are the palest
most tender of pink

★★★

a rainbow arches round her
moving with her when she moves

she is a woman
who has found her beginning

the wistfulness of water
mist in the narrows

a sacred place

★★★

she has lost her words   searches for them everywhere
in the mouths of family and friends   *ahh ahh*
she says when one of them escapes again   *ahh*
I help her look   give her some of mine
she borrows them gratefully   the speech therapist
loans her his too   at least the beginnings so she can find
     the ends

this is a pretty bunch of *fl fl* he says pointing to the picture
flowers she laughs clapping her hands   *flowers*
I want to give them to her in celebration   a whole armful
of flowers   masses of them   because she has finally found
     the word
I want to give her the word for everything   flowers and
     puppies
and Christmas trees   and this one   I give her this one
     family

★★★

the coyote in the field is *papaya*
slippery ice is *itchy*
my slip on shoes are *coupons*

I tell her she is becoming a poet
no she says and hugs me *you*

★★★

a voice now tarnished
o to see her again shining

to hear her mind untrammelled
and singing all the old songs

to have her music
poured like living silver
gleaming in the polished light

★★★

stones speak to my sister
she is chosen by stones
they call out to her
she answers them

cupped in her palm
a stone egg blood warm
she touches to that tender hollow
at the base of her throat

stones speak to my sister
their smooth articulations
they whisper to her
the colours of earth
texture of sunlight

taste she tells me
a pebble peppermint white
cool as breath

listen she says
to the hush of stones
the cadence of their language
is time is patience

stones speak to my sister
they bring her comfort
the warm weight of their peace

2

patience is the wideness of the night
the simple pain of stars

Phyllis Webb

the bitter night so wide
so filled with lost things

from deep in the woods deer drift
to the lip of the clearing

they are here then gone

the moment struck like vespers bell

there are lessons
if I will only learn them

★★★

resting our heads
on one another's shoulders
we lean into each other
as horses do
in winter storms

we have known
the great heartache of horses
she and I
when all around us

it was coming down hard

together we've withstood
the worst of weather
sometimes the snow
so thick we could not see

in our nearness we have found peace
the simple grace of horses
laying their great heads
on one another's shoulders

everything whispers now of time
we gentle one another
around us the slow snow falling

***

this December morning
we are walking along the old Shellbrook highway
not so much a highway anymore
 as a trail through the trees
the traffic all keeps to the new road
everyone going somewhere in a hurry
but not us we are in no rush
there is nothing but time for my sister now
no flights to catch no appointments of importance
her smart business suits traded in
for t-shirts and comfortable pants
she walks in the snow now in her new red boots

shows me the fretwork tracks of rabbits
listen she says as we stop
to hear the chatter of chickadees
the clean wind as it lifts and sighs
delighted she hugs the day holds it out to me
the deer she knows and morning sun
and winter days and joy   my sister's gifts

and this is what matters now
this slow walk with my sister on this soft morning
having her here beside me in her red boots
the sound of her quiet breathing   snow in the pines

★★★

I would give her silence
wrapped in soft cloth
quiet as flannel
she could touch to her cheek
hold it close
when the world's clatter
is too much with her

she could unfold that silence
and find inside
the forest's deep hush
be there among the tall cool trees
in the deepening shadows
the delicate movements of deer
I would give her solitude

an aloneness which is not lonely
but a gift of rest

for her I would make the world move quietly
give her the slow gold of a sunset
lingering over the lake
the lisp of water at the shore

these gentle rhythms
I would give her
the soft brush of a breath
in the deep stillness of snow

***

she wants me to
needs me to say
goodbye   hello
to this new sister
sweet soul
I wasn't ready for

vespers bell
all will be well
it tells me

now is a time to be

***

she flows
towards a destination
she cannot know
this river she is
that borders rock and sky
moving from what has vanished
to what remains
this slow unwinding
that re-forms re-makes
in the dark water of her reflection
a new moon rises
and in the morning
rinsed with light
she shines

verge 8

I dream the wild violet
scent of you
the red gold russet quick
blaze of you
through the trees
waiting at the water's edge

I dream you
shape shifter
woman   fox   woman
you are me   I you

I dream the small bells
of your ears
pricked and listening

I am on the verge
of some understanding
some thing I am meant to know ...

after the biopsy

that little lump she tells me
could be a grief bubbling up
since it's above your heart

grief does that she says
like those little bubbles that rise up
from the bottom of a stream
where the weeds have rotted

something dies
there's always the evidence
on the surface at some point

you have to start all over again
it's a big space left behind
fill it with tears she tells me
lots of things can live in salty water

voice

the quieter you become,
the more you can hear
Ram Dass

there is a voice to the small stones
a voice to the small specks of stars
the sun speaks of laughter
the tall grass talks
of its love affair with wind
and the sticks of driftwood say
it is as good to be a stick
of driftwood merry in the little eddies

as it was good once
to be a willow bough
or the branch of some great tree

knowing

in the autumn field were four horses
one tall and reddish gold and regal
there was a plump white mare
and two painted ponies
full of all kinds of fire

I went to the wire fence then
called out to them
and they came racing across
in a river of flying manes and hoof beats
nuzzling my pockets for apples
touching their wide gentle faces right up to mine
looking right into me   their eyes so dark and soft

they seemed to know me
I can't explain it any other way
for the longest time I stood there
telling them how beautiful they were
everything seemed to slow down
they made me weep   they were so perfectly themselves

I want to know what those horses know
to understand that quiet simplicity
that deep trust that lives in them
the good hearted grace of a horse

this small longing

walking the trail to the trout pond
one early April evening
I come across a young doe
grazing the new grass
she lifts her head to gaze at me

the light from her dark eyes
is the kind the vanished sun leaves
all mystery and distance

the birds   the wind
have gone suddenly still
as if everything stops for her
even time

she moves across my path
with a slow elegance
then she is gone and I am left
with this small longing
the grace of her goodbye

verge 9

tonight
little truth teller
you wait until your thoughts
take shape
and then you say
what shape that is
to the slender moon

I look at you
and see freedom
I listen
and yours are the best words
the heart can speak

so wild and beautiful it is
this way of seeing
satori — a sudden re-seeing of things ...

nobody told me

that clove coloured paint
could change my kitchen
from bland to beautiful
that's all it would take
to make such a difference

I painted us in all the wrong colours
with a brush of my own making
and turned us too many bitter blues
too many shades of sadness
the hazy greys or winter whites
I've made us in the past

I've painted us poorly
in unflattering tones
that did nothing
for who we were in any light

I'm discovering
it's all in the colour you choose

nest

this nest she finds in the forest
abandoned or raven raided
just a bundle of sticks
like me she thinks
a bundle of doubts and second thoughts

a nest of no eggs   of nothingness
a catch basin for her emptiness

she looks at the nest
thinks about the missing eggs
but slowly she starts to see
the intricate basket for what it is

the twigs and leaves
their undersides so delicately woven
like a moment of understanding
that comes out of nowhere small and bright

she cups the nest in her two hands
carries it so carefully home

lingua

my heart speaks a shockwave stutter
inside me a frantic
flutter of hummingbird words
slurred syllables of loon song
in a tongue I don't want to know

I'd rather Spanish
the lingua of passion and flowers
the memory my body holds
of smoke and swirling skirts
Mijas that little mountain town
sun brilliant on white adobe walls

I want a language of far away places
far from these ice white walls
from this antiseptic doctor talk
chilled as I am needled and shivering
under this too thin hospital blanket

in this place only your eyes
and the touch of your hand lull me
a familiar long known language
the love that enters softly
into my blood's current
and speaks to my yammering heart

new again

May and the surprise of marsh marigolds
tickling the sides of a small stream
young poplars with their lime coloured leaves
trembling in a tender breeze

the ice only a week gone
and the lake so still the sky lives in it

at sunset two leggy sandpipers preen
on the strand of beach
while carnelian lights up
the underside of clouds
like a made-for-movies heaven

and later still stars all tangled
in the tops of the blue spruce
the loon's distant tremolo
and on the night air the tang of pine
and loam and lake water

everything is new again
my skin listens glistening

path

once my breath
hung in the air
ragged
I ran through forests
calling out to the trees

in starlight
I was a dark shadow moving
against the birches
their silver arms reaching
always wishing for the moon

enough of grief
I am done so done with sadness
this too dark path
cutting through the chilled night air
enough of shade   of all this blue

through dappled
and dancing patterns of green
I catch a glimpse of joy
on a gull's white wing

this kind of love

it's a gift of stars you share together or a full moon
fat as October   it's the warm bread smell of your infant son
the sashes thrown open to ribbons of sunlight   full of
    colours
helpless laughter and deepest sorrowing   it's in the love note
of her hair across your pillow

it's a promise   a wish   in the word contentment   the
    word peace
it forgives and forgives this kind of love
it's being found when you've been lost and alone
and someone bundles you in blankets
and says you're safe now   you're safe

it has its own angels   this kind of love
it has wings to carry you home

these waning days

late August kids gone back to the city   end of season sales
dark now at nine   a slow sweet melancholy to these
     shorter days
gulls huddle along the barren beach   lake gunmetal gray
wind torn whitecaps momentarily lit by a shaft of sun

at night I light candles   write at the old wood table
with a glass of wine and music turned low
I curve into these hours   fit perfectly into their slow
     unwinding
 time so deep here it runs over me   through me
 I find here something I need   wrap it around me
soft as the shawl my sister-in-law sent
for when you're writing at the cabin

soon the poplars will be painted by September frost
geese pass in concert   bull elk bugling beneath the
     northern lights
soon time to close the cottage for another year
but for now I savour this time I have
to move with these waning days   the slow pendulum's
     swing

through the dark murmur of trees

In the forests of Japan, the spirits of suicide
leave through the dark murmur of trees
                    from *Tree Notes* by Laura Lush

through the dark murmur of pines
I heard you leaving
echo of your laughter
startled I turned
to find you gone

you spoke   my brother
into the high bare branches
of the winter trees
your voice rising
through the pale arms
of the paper birch
where the music of you
stays written
where there will always be
your song

song

in the crisp quiet
at Kinasao if you listen carefully
the lake ice sings to the pines
to the low winter sky
into the core of me
lone woman standing on the frozen shore

the lake sings all the old songs
of love and longing
the songs I know so well
that sit in my hurt heart
where they live with their quiet humming

it sings of my sister
shaping a new path
of that list I keep of old losses
mother father brother friends
lining up their familiar faces
mourning each of their domino deaths

it sings the questions
that quicken inside of me
who am I what am I doing here
songs that puzzle under the lake ice
and move across
the constant white ache of snow

at Kinasao the lake sings
and here I am able to listen
to let that song ring out
the clear true notes
rising up and out
over the tops of blue spruce
and tamarack that touch the shore

and it's all of our songs
and each of us singing
as the lake does
of what moves beneath
the sheet glass surface of things

verge 10

silence out here in the still woods
where I stop to rest against a toppled poplar
I listen   only Max huffing after a squirrel
the sough of wind through the pine boughs

I can almost catch the distant dance of the river
that runs below carved deep into the forest floor
can almost feel it moving along
the day slipping past
just a short walk away
the road with its ribbon of traffic

but here   small fox   each moment is as the one before
I wait in the forest's calm heart
the past so easy now for all its pain
the trees know the future
deep in their rhythmic sleeping

patient as these pines I want to be
like you   unhurried and graceful
accepting of what comes next

Acknowledgements

I am grateful to Dave Margoshes for his deft and perceptive editing and whose insightful questions helped me walk more deeply into the poems. To Michael Mirolla and Guernica Editions for believing in *verge*. A huge thanks to Jan Wood who showed me the fox needed to run through the forest, and to the members of Sans Nom Poetry group, good friends and fine poets all – Carla Braidek, Veryl Coghill, Beth Gobeil, Kim Kuzak, Sharon Bird, Laurie Muirhead, Rod Thompson, Jan Wood, Denise Wilkinson and Joy McCall. And always much love and thanks to my incredible family. You are my greatest gift.

The author would like to acknowledge the following publications in which many of these poems appeared: *The Society, Room, The Toronto Quarterly, The Oral Tradition, The Windsor Review, Transition, Antigonish Review, Barefoot Review, Prairie Fire*, the anthologies *Untying the Apron* and *Skating in the Exit Light*. Several poetry sequences were also previously broadcast on CBC Radio's *SoundXchange* program. Thanks also to the Saskatchewan Arts Board for financial support during the writing of these poems.

Song lyrics in "the ironing" from "Rose" by Rod McKuen, 1960

About the Author

Lynda Monahan is the author of two previous collections of poetry, *A Slow Dance in the Flames* and *What My Body Knows*, both published by Coteau Books. Her work has appeared in a number of Canadian literary magazines and broadcast on CBC radio. She has taught creative writing at SIAST Woodland Campus in Prince Albert, Saskatchewan, for the past several years and facilitates a variety of writing workshops for schools and organizations across the province. She compiled and edited *Second Chances: the stories of acquired brain injury survivors* for the Saskatchewan Acquired Brain Injury Association. She was the managing editor of Spring Volume IV, Windscript, a mentor in the Artsmart Youth Mentorship program, and the facilitator for the Sage Hill Teen Writing Experience in both Saskatoon and Prince Albert. She was writer-in-residence at Balfour Collegiate and for the Saskatchewan Writers Guild facilitated retreat. Currently she is writer on the wards at the Victoria Hospital and facilitates a Writing For Your Life group with the Canadian Mental Health Association. She lives in the Nesbit Forest just outside of the city of Prince Albert, Saskatchewan, with her husband, Don.

RECYCLED
Paper made from
recycled material
FSC® C100212

Printed in December 2014
by Gauvin Press,
Gatineau, Québec